FREE MASK

You Will Need:

- Thin elastic, wool or string

- Scissors

- Sticky Tape

Instructions:

1. Pull out the mask page.
2. Pop out the mask.
3. Cut enough elastic/wool/string to fit around the back of your head.
4. Attach to the back of the mask with some sticky tape.
5. Have fun with your new mask!

SCISSORS ARE SHARP! ASK AN ADULT FOR HELP BEFORE USING.

CONTENTS

STAR WARS™

Published 2013. Pedigree Books Limited, Beech Hill House, Walnut Gardens, Exeter, Devon EX4 4DH.
www.pedigreebooks.com – books@pedigreegroup.co.uk
The Pedigree trademark, email and website addresses, are the sole and exclusive properties
of Pedigree Group Limited, used under licence in this publication.

The Galactic Republic has governed the galaxy for over 25 thousand years, but it has become weak and corrupt. Many senators are greedy, with no interest in the common good. It is becoming more difficult for the Jedi to maintain peace in the galaxy.

Meanwhile, on a distant planet, the destiny of a simple slave boy is entangled with the future of the galaxy. A chain of events has begun that will one day lead to the destruction of the Republic itself.

The galaxy is about to enter its darkest time...

DROID ARMY

THE DROID ARMY HAS INVADED YOUR ANNUAL! TEN DROIDS ARE LURKING AMONG THE PAGES. PUT A TICK BESIDE EACH DROID AS YOU FIND IT.

CHARACTER CROSSWORD

This puzzle will challenge your intelligence and your powers of observation. There are ten names to fit into this [gri]d. First solve the clues, and [t]hen figure out where they [b]elong in the grid. Good luck!

The Chosen One

The first name of the Queen of Naboo during the Trade Federation blockade

The oldest member of the Jedi Council

A cyborg general

Darth _ _ _ _ _ _ _, Sith Master

The Jedi Master who taught Obi-Wan Kenobi

A clumsy Gungan

Ki-_ _ _ -Mundi

The clone marshal commander assigned to Obi-Wan Kenobi during the Clone Wars

A Wookiee hero of the Clone Wars

"The fear of loss is a path to the dark side."

FAST FACTS

SPECIES: Unknown

HOMEWORLD: Unknown

HEIGHT: 0.66m

LOYALTY: Jedi

FRIENDS: Mace Windu, Obi-Wan Kenobi

ENEMIES: Count Dooku

WEAPON

NAME: Lightsaber

COLOUR: Green

DESCRIPTION:
This blade of pure energy can cut through almost anything. It takes years of practice to learn how to use a lightsaber well, and each one is different. A Jedi makes his or her own weapon as part of their training.

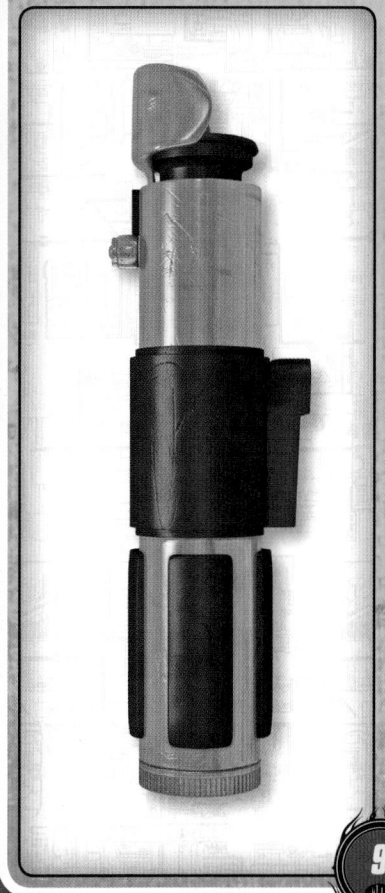

YODA

Yoda is the oldest and wisest member of the Jedi Council. He has trained countless Younglings and Padawans in the ways of the Force. He has a strong connection to the Force, and he speaks in a way that is both simple and powerful.

No one knows Yoda's age exactly, but he has been alive for over 800 years. In that time, he has visited countless worlds in his quest to understand and connect with the Force. His experience and understanding have earned him great respect.

THE CLONE WARS

The Sith had waited for many years to take their revenge on the Jedi. As the Old Republic weakened, the lords of the dark side seized their chance.

The ruling Senate was full of greedy, weak and petty politicians. Darth Sidious knew that he could control them. He made long-term plans to destroy the democratic Republic from within. His aim was to start a war that would engulf the galaxy.

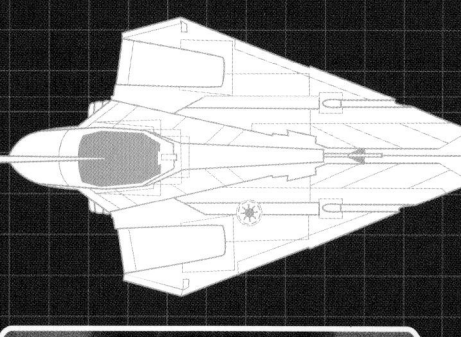

Darth Sidious's Plan

1. Make an alliance with forces of commerce who have droid armies, like the Trade Federation.
2. Create a clone army that will be loyal to the Republic.
3. Instruct Darth Tyranus to form a Separatist movement, made up of star systems that want to leave the Republic.
4. Lure the Jedi into a trap so they are forced to use the clone army and start a war.
5. Wait for the turmoil of war to weaken the galaxy.
6. Order the clone army to destroy the Jedi.

The Clone Wars began, and conflict swept across the galaxy. Heroes and villains were made and destroyed in each new battle. The Jedi had always been the defenders of peace. Now they were forced to fight.

Master Yoda sent Jedi Knights to many different planets and star systems. Their orders were to do everything they could to weaken the Separatists. That included organising and training secret opposition groups.

The Clone Wars came to a blood-soaked end when the clone army was given Order 66: Kill all Jedi. Darth Vader wiped out the Separatist Council on Mustafar, and the Emperor took command of the galaxy.

Major Conflict Sites

Geonosis

Kamino

Naboo

STAR WARS
EPISODE I
THE PHANTOM MENACE

"The Federation has gone too far this time."
Queen Amidala

When the Trade Federation used their battleships to cut off the planet of Naboo, the Supreme Chancellor sent two Jedi Knights to try to solve the problem.

Qui-Gon Jinn and Obi-Wan Kenobi expected to be treated with respect by Nute Gunray, the Viceroy of the Trade Federation. But the viceroy was following the orders of a Sith Lord called Darth Sidious, who wanted the Jedi dead!

Obi-Wan and Qui-Gon escaped and made friends with a clumsy but kind Gungan called Jar Jar Binks. Together, they travelled underwater to warn Queen Amidala.

"There's always a bigger fish."
Qui-Gon Jinn

The Queen was captured, but the Jedi rescued her and her handmaidens. They escaped on her personal starship, heading for Coruscant so that she could ask the Senate for help.

When he heard what had happened, Darth Sidious ordered his apprentice, Darth Maul, to recapture the Queen.

"No one can kill a Jedi."
Anakin Skywalker

The starship's hyperdrive was leaking, so they had to land on a planet called Tatooine. Qui-Gon Jinn found replacement parts in a junk shop, but he had no money.

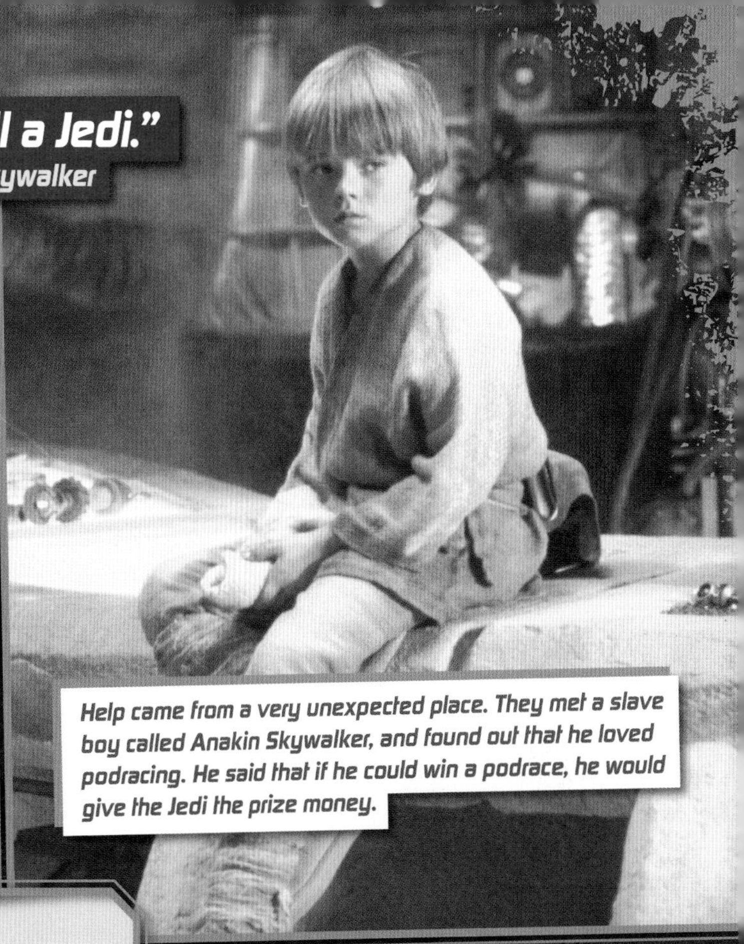

Help came from a very unexpected place. They met a slave boy called Anakin Skywalker, and found out that he loved podracing. He said that if he could win a podrace, he would give the Jedi the prize money.

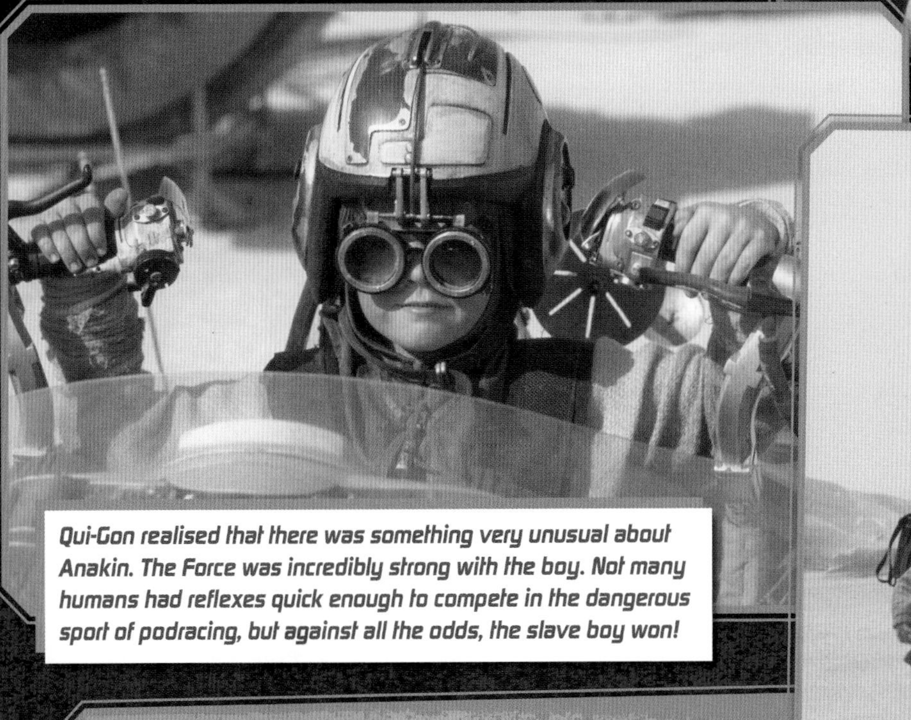

Qui-Gon realised that there was something very unusual about Anakin. The Force was incredibly strong with the boy. Not many humans had reflexes quick enough to compete in the dangerous sport of podracing, but against all the odds, the slave boy won!

Qui-Gon bought the parts for the ship and freed Anakin from slavery. He wanted to take Anakin to Coruscant and train him as a Jedi.

As the ship left the desert planet, Darth Maul found them. He attacked Qui-Gon, but he couldn't stop the ship from leaving.

"Fear leads to anger;
anger leads to hate;
hate leads to suffering."
Master Yoda

13

> ### "Clouded this boy's future is."
> Master Yoda

On the way to Coruscant, Anakin became good friends with a girl called Padmé, whom he believed to be one of the Queen's handmaidens.

Qui-Gon was sure that Anakin was the Chosen One mentioned in ancient prophecy. However, the Jedi Council saw that the boy's future was clouded by fear and refused to train him. Qui-Gon was very disappointed. He vowed to train Anakin himself.

> ### "You will be a Jedi. I promise."
> Obi-Wan Kenobi

The Senate was so divided by petty arguments that no one could agree to help Naboo. Senator Palpatine thought that Naboo needed a strong leader, and persuaded Queen Amidala to call for a vote of no confidence in Supreme Chancellor Valorum.

Queen Amidala decided to return home, and was in the company of the Jedi Knights, Anakin, Jar Jar and her handmaidens. But Darth Sidious sent Darth Maul to Naboo as well.

On Naboo, the Queen visited Jar Jar's leader, Boss Nass. But Padmé stepped forward. She was the real Queen! And she had a plan.

Padmé persuaded Boss Nass to join forces to fight the invasion. While the Gungan army decoyed the droid army away from the capital city, Padmé's pilots went to attack the droid control ship in space.

"Your focus determines your reality."
Qui-Gon Jinn

While the Jedi fought Darth Maul, Padmé took her team into the palace to find the viceroy and Anakin hid inside a starfighter. The Jedi were too busy with Darth Maul to notice what the little boy was doing. He accidentally turned on the starfighter and blasted off. Anakin was joining the fight in space!

To Obi-Wan's horror, Darth Maul thrust his lightsaber through Qui-Gon's body. Obi-Wan defeated Darth Maul, but he couldn't save his Master. There was only one thing he could do for Qui-Gon. He promised to train Anakin as a Jedi.

Anakin had managed to fly into the space station hangar. He fired his torpedoes into the reactor. The ship started to explode!

"At last we will reveal ourselves to the Jedi. At last we will have our revenge."
Darth Maul

Without the control ship, the droids on the planet stopped working. The war was won! But Darth Sidious was still lurking in the shadows, and there were dark times ahead for the Republic.

STAR WARS
EPISODE II
ATTACK OF THE CLONES

> "I will not let this Republic that has stood for a thousand years be split in two."
> *Palpatine*

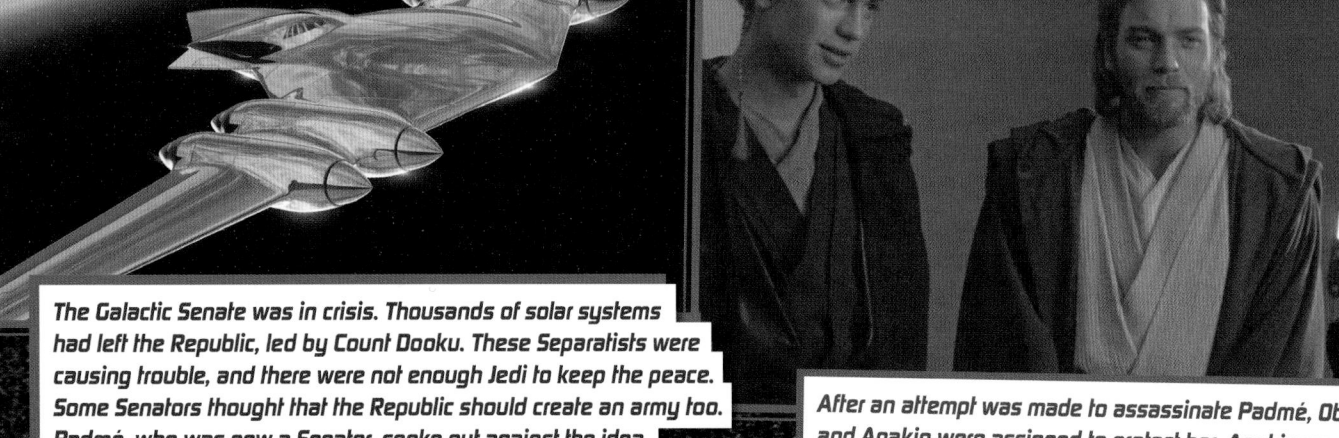

The Galactic Senate was in crisis. Thousands of solar systems had left the Republic, led by Count Dooku. These Separatists were causing trouble, and there were not enough Jedi to keep the peace. Some Senators thought that the Republic should create an army too. Padmé, who was now a Senator, spoke out against the idea.

After an attempt was made to assassinate Padmé, Obi-Wan and Anakin were assigned to protect her. Anakin was excited, because he hadn't seen Padmé for ten years.

He and Obi-Wan foiled a midnight attack on the Senator, and finally caught up with the assassin in the dark streets of Coruscant.

> "Just being around her again is intoxicating."
> *Anakin Skywalker*

On the journey, Anakin and Padmé shared stories and told each other their hopes and fears. They grew to be close friends.

"We're keepers of the peace, not soldiers."
Mace Windu

Obi-Wan's friend Dex told him that the toxic dart was made on Kamino, beyond the Outer Rim. Kaminoans were cloners, and Obi-Wan had never heard of the planet before.

On Kamino, Obi-Wan was amazed to find that his visit was expected. The Kaminoans had used a bounty hunter called Jango Fett to create a clone army, following orders that they believed came from the Republic. Jango Fett was raising one of the clones as his son, Boba. Was Jango the bounty hunter who had hired Zam Wesell?

Obi-Wan followed Jango Fett to Geonosis, where he found Count Dooku and the Separatists. They had a huge army of battle droids and were ready for war. Obi-Wan was captured as he was sending a message to Anakin.

On Naboo, Anakin's time with Padmé was spoiled by dreams that his mother was in danger. He went to Tatooine with Padmé and R2-D2.

"Be mindful of your thoughts, Anakin, they betray you."
Obi-Wan Kenobi

Tusken Raiders had kidnapped Anakin's mother. He was too late to save her, and she died in his arms. Giving in to his anger, he killed every single Tusken Raider in the camp.

17

Anakin and Padmé sent Obi-Wan's message to the Jedi Council and then set a course for Geonosis.

On Coruscant, the Senators voted to give Supreme Chancellor Palpatine special emergency powers. This meant that he could make fast decisions during the Separatist crisis. Straight away, he approved the use of the clone army.

Padmé and Anakin arrived on Geonosis and tried to find Obi-Wan, but they were captured. The Separatists decided to execute them in an arena with Obi-Wan Kenobi, before an audience of cheering crowds. Believing that they were about to die, Anakin and Padmé exchanged vows of true love.

"This party's over."
Mace Windu

The prisoners faced three snarling monsters, and the Separatist leaders waited eagerly to see them torn to pieces. But the Separatists had underestimated the Jedi and the Senator. The beasts were defeated!

At that moment, all around the arena, dozens of lightsabers were ignited. There were many Jedi Knights in the crowd! Droid soldiers poured into the arena, and so began the Battle of Geonosis.

18

Lightsabers lit up the arena as the outnumbered Jedi fought for their lives. Many droid soldiers were destroyed and Mace Windu beheaded Jango Fett, but it was only a matter of time before the sheer number of droids defeated them.

Then, in an instant, everything changed. A fleet of gunships swooped out of the sky under the command of Master Yoda. It was the army of the Republic!

Soon the droid army was retreating, and Count Dooku decided to leave. Obi-Wan and Anakin tried to stop him, but he was a skilled and experienced warrior. Obi-Wan was knocked out and Anakin lost an arm. Dooku turned to leave, but Master Yoda was waiting for him.

It was a fierce and fast duel. For all his style and skill, Dooku could not match Yoda's ability with a lightsaber. Instead, he distracted the wise old Jedi with an attack on Obi-Wan and Anakin. Dooku escaped while Yoda helped his friends.

During the weeks that followed, the Chancellor requested thousands more clone troopers from Kamino. Anakin and Padmé were secretly married, and the Jedi Knights faced the fact that the galaxy was at war.

"The shroud of the dark side has fallen. Begun...the Clone War has."
Master Yoda

19

BIOGRAPHY FILES

FAST FACTS

SPECIES: Human

HOMEWORLD: Stewjon

HEIGHT: 1.79m

LOYALTY: Jedi

FRIENDS: Anakin Skywalker, Yoda

ENEMIES: General Grievous, Count Dooku

VEHICLE

NAME: ETA-2 Jedi Starfighter

SIZE: 5.47m

TOP SPEED: 1500 kph

WEAPONS: 2 dual laser cannons, 2 ion cannons

CREW: 1 pilot, 1 astromech droid

OBI-WAN KENOBI

"My allegiance is to the Republic."

Obi-Wan Kenobi is a Jedi Master who is also a General in the Clone Wars. He is patient and cautious, although he has learned from his Padawan Anakin that being impetuous can sometimes pay off!

Obi-Wan Kenobi is a master of a lightsaber fighting style called Ataru, in which defence is more important than attack. However, there is another style called Soresu, which needs both patience and daring. Soresu is the style of fighting most suited to Obi-Wan's character.

SPOT THE DIFFERENCE

Look carefully at these two pictures of Anakin and Padmé in Watto's shop. Can you find ten differences between them?

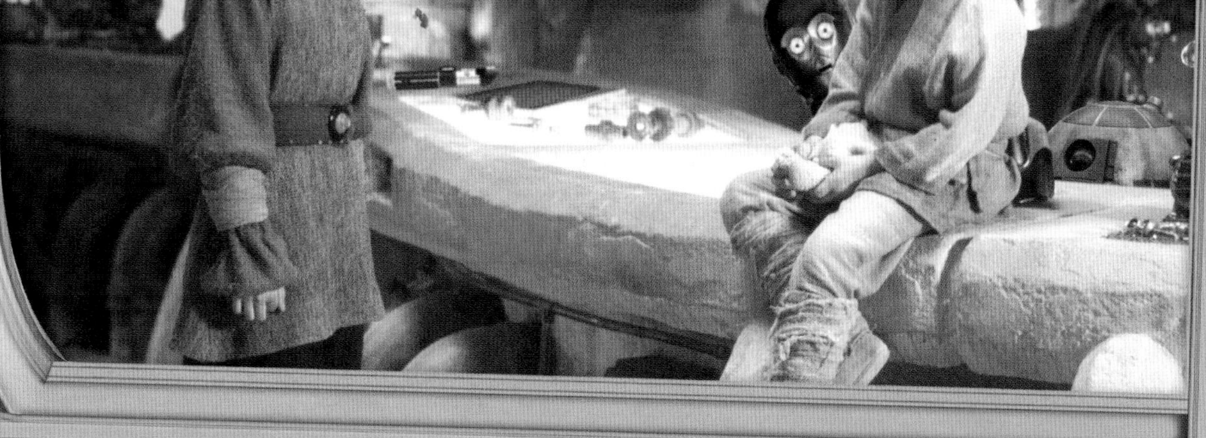

CHOOSE YOUR SIDE

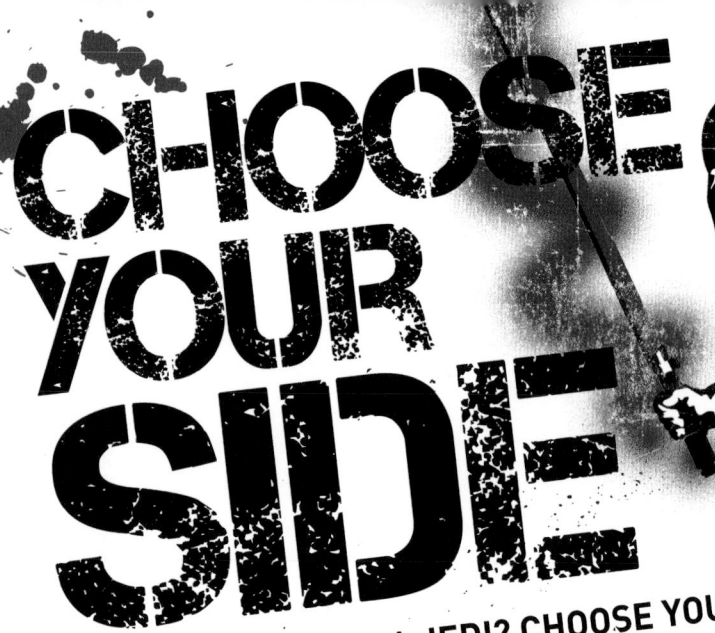

ARE YOU A SITH OR A JEDI? CHOOSE YOUR SIDE AND THEN COLLECT EVERYTHING YOU'LL NEED TO DESIGN YOUR OWN T-SHIRT.

1. CUT ALONG THE DOTTED LINE ON THE OPPOSITE PAGE TO REMOVE YOUR CHOSEN DESIGN FROM THE BOOK.

2. Using a craft knife or scissors, carefully cut out all the black areas to make the stencil holes.

3. Tape your stencil to the card using masking tape. Then cut out a stronger stencil from the card.

4. USE MASKING TAPE TO ATTACH THE STENCIL TO THE FRONT OF YOUR T-SHIRT.

5. Paint through the stencil onto your T-shirt, making sure you cover all the holes.

6. SLOWLY AND GENTLY PEEL AWAY THE STENCIL. THEN WAIT FOR THE PAINT TO DRY.

7. If your paint needs to be fixed using an iron, follow the instructions on the packet. Cover the paint with a cloth to stop it sticking to the iron.

USE THE FORCE

The Dark Side

ASK AN ADULT TO HELP YOU WHEN USING SCISSORS AND AN IRON.

USE THE FORCE

The Dark Side

The Politics of the Galaxy

The Galactic Republic was a democratic collection of star systems that ruled the galaxy for millennia. The Jedi Order defended the Republic, working with the Force to maintain balance.

Each star system in the Republic elected a Senator to represent them. These Senators ruled from the Senate Chamber on Coruscant.

There were millions of worlds in the Republic, and by working together they achieved peace in the galaxy. It was a system built on tolerance and respect of other species.

However, as time passed, some of the planets' representatives became corrupt and greedy. It grew harder for the Supreme Chancellor to control the Senate, which was bogged down in complicated paperwork and petty squabbles.

This weakness gave the Sith a chance to seize control. Senator Palpatine became the Supreme Chancellor, and slowly took power by amending the constitution. He was careful to make the changes gradually, so it seemed as if they were the only option.

Only when the time was right did he reveal his true identity as a Dark Lord of the Sith. With the help of Anakin Skywalker and the clone army, he wiped out most of the Jedi Order. Then he told the Senate that the Jedi were traitors, and revealed his plan to establish the Galactic Empire.

Symbol of the Force

During the Clone Wars, all Republic vehicles were marked with a symbol of a disc with eight spokes. This was an ancient icon that stood for the presence of the Force in the galaxy. After the fall of the Galactic Republic, the Emperor personalised the symbol by removing two of the spokes.

At the Battle of Coruscant, Anakin Skywalker's starfighter was the only Jedi vehicle to carry the symbol with six spokes.

FAST FACTS

SPECIES: Wookiee

HOMEWORLD: Kashyyyk

HEIGHT: 2.29m

LOYALTY: Republic

FRIENDS: Yoda, Tarfful

WEAPON

NAME: Bowcaster

SIZE: 77.4cm

RANGE: 30m (optimal), 50m (maximum)

CAPACITY: 6 quarrels per load, 100 shots from gas cartridge, 200 shots from power charge

FUNCTIONS: Quarrel autofeed mechanism, automatic recocking system.

DESCRIPTION: A laser crossbow that fires energy quarrels or explosive arrows.

CHEWBACCA

The Wookiee warrior Chewbacca is loyal, intelligent and very strong. He has served under the command of Jedi Master Yoda since Separatist forces invaded his beloved homeworld Kashyyyk.

Like all Wookiees, Chewbacca is known for his bravery and ferocity. He and his fellow warrior Tarfful stand ready to protect Kashyyyk from droid invasion. He has great respect for Master Yoda, who knows that the loyalty of a Wookiee is a valuable thing.

"It's not wise to upset a Wookiee."

25

MAP OF DESTINY

The Force guides the lives of everyone in the galaxy, whether they know it or not. Can you see into the future? Look at each of these characters and fill in their names. Then complete the destinies that the Force has mapped out for them.

1

g_ _ _ - _ _ _ _   _ _ _

His most famous Padawan will be _____.

He will discover a very special boy on the planet _____.

He will die at the hands of _____.

2

_ _ _ _ _   _ _ _ _ _ _

He will sit on the Jedi Council with _____.

He will have an unusual _____lightsaber.

He will die at the hands of _____.

3

_ - _ _ _ - _ _ _   _ _ _ _ _ _ _

He will kill _____.

He will die at the hands of _____.

He will watch over _____'s son.

4

— — — — — — — —

He will spend the first years of his life on _____.

He will see _____kill his father.

He will become a _____.

5

— — — — — — — — — — — — —

She will become Queen of _____.

She will get _____in secret.

Her daughter will be brought up by _____.

6

— — — — — — — — — — —

He will help to save the lives of several _____.

He will help _____'s Padawan after Order 66.

He will die when his _____explodes.

7

— — — —

He will lose a battle with _____.

He will train _____'s son to be a Jedi.

He will become one with the Force on the planet of _____.

8

— — — — — — — — — — — — — — —

He will bring _____to the Force.

He will help stop an assassin sent by _____'s father.

He will kill the _____in the Temple.

EYE-DENTITY PARADE

You're being watched! To be a good Jedi like Yoda you need to quickly recognise friends and enemies. Look carefully at these eyes and name the character who owns them.

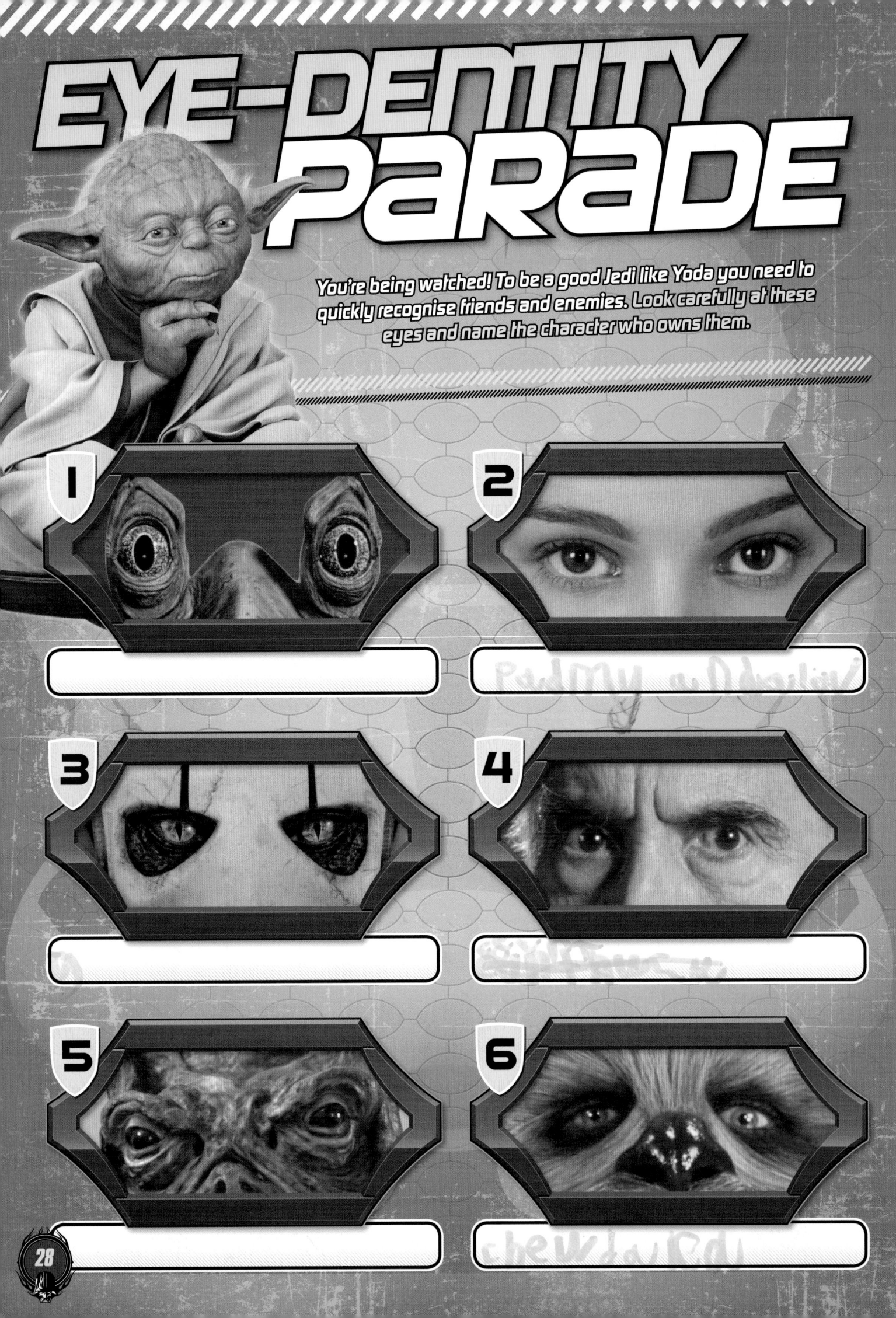

1

2

Podmy Doglow

3

4

5

6

chewbaied

FAST FACTS

SPECIES:	Human
HOMEWORLD:	Haruun Kal
HEIGHT:	1.88m
LOYALTY:	Jedi Council
FRIENDS:	Depa Billaba, Master Yoda
ENEMIES:	Gorm the Dissolver

WEAPON

NAME:	Lightsaber
COLOUR:	Purple

DESCRIPTION: According to legend, Mace Windu collected the crystals for his unique lightsaber when he was just 14 years old. It has an electrum finish and its hilt is 0.28m long. Plo Koon and Luminara Unduli have lightsabers with exactly the same hilt.

"We're keepers of the peace, not soldiers."

MACE WINDU

Mace Windu is a remarkable Jedi Master. He is a fearsome warrior and yet he prefers peace. His cool, calm manner of speaking makes him seem overly disciplined to some, but he also has a quirky sense of humour that only his friends ever see.

Mace Windu invented the Vaapad fighting technique, and is a master of all Jedi fighting styles. He can see 'shatterpoints' – the moments or actions that will cause his enemies to break.

As an orphan, his earliest memories are of Yoda, who found him on Haruun Kal. He joined the Jedi Council at the age of 28, and only three opponents have ever defeated him in battle – Master Yoda, Count Dooku and Darth Sidious.

STAR WARS
EPISODE III
REVENGE OF THE SITH

PART 1

Times were hard for the galaxy. Three years of war had brought pain and suffering to many planets. Now, disaster had struck the Republic. General Grievous had kidnapped Supreme Chancellor Palpatine, and without him the Senate was in uproar. Obi-Wan and Anakin were sent to rescue Palpatine from General Grievous's ship, the Invisible Hand.

It seemed impossible even to reach the ship, but Obi-Wan and Anakin fought their way through laser attacks, vulture droids and enemy fighters.

It was three years since Obi-Wan and Anakin had last duelled Dooku, and since then they had grown greatly in skill. Obi-Wan was knocked out, but Anakin blazed with energy and power. He cut off Dooku's hands and seized his red lightsaber.

"I've been looking forward to this."
Count Dooku

At last Anakin and Obi-Wan boarded the Invisible Hand and located the Chancellor. He had been imprisoned on the observation platform. Before they could release him, Count Dooku entered the room.

Urged on by Palpatine, Anakin beheaded his unarmed prisoner. Then he picked up Obi-Wan, even though the Chancellor wanted to leave him behind.

"Kill him now!"
Palpatine

"His fate will be the same as ours."
Anakin Skywalker

"Time to abandon ship."
General Greviuos

General Grievous would not let the Chancellor go so easily. Wielding electrostaffs, his bodyguards attacked the Jedi. Electrical bolts flew around as the ship began to fall apart under enemy fire. General Grievous left the Jedi for dead and headed for the escape pods.

General Grievous left the Jedi with no means of escape, but Anakin used the Force to control the ship and land safely on Coruscant.

"This is a happy moment. The happiest moment of my life."
Anakin Skywalker

It was months since he had seen Padmé, and he was overjoyed to find that she was going to have a baby.

But soon his happiness was spoiled by disturbing dreams that she would die in childbirth. He was haunted by his fear of losing her.

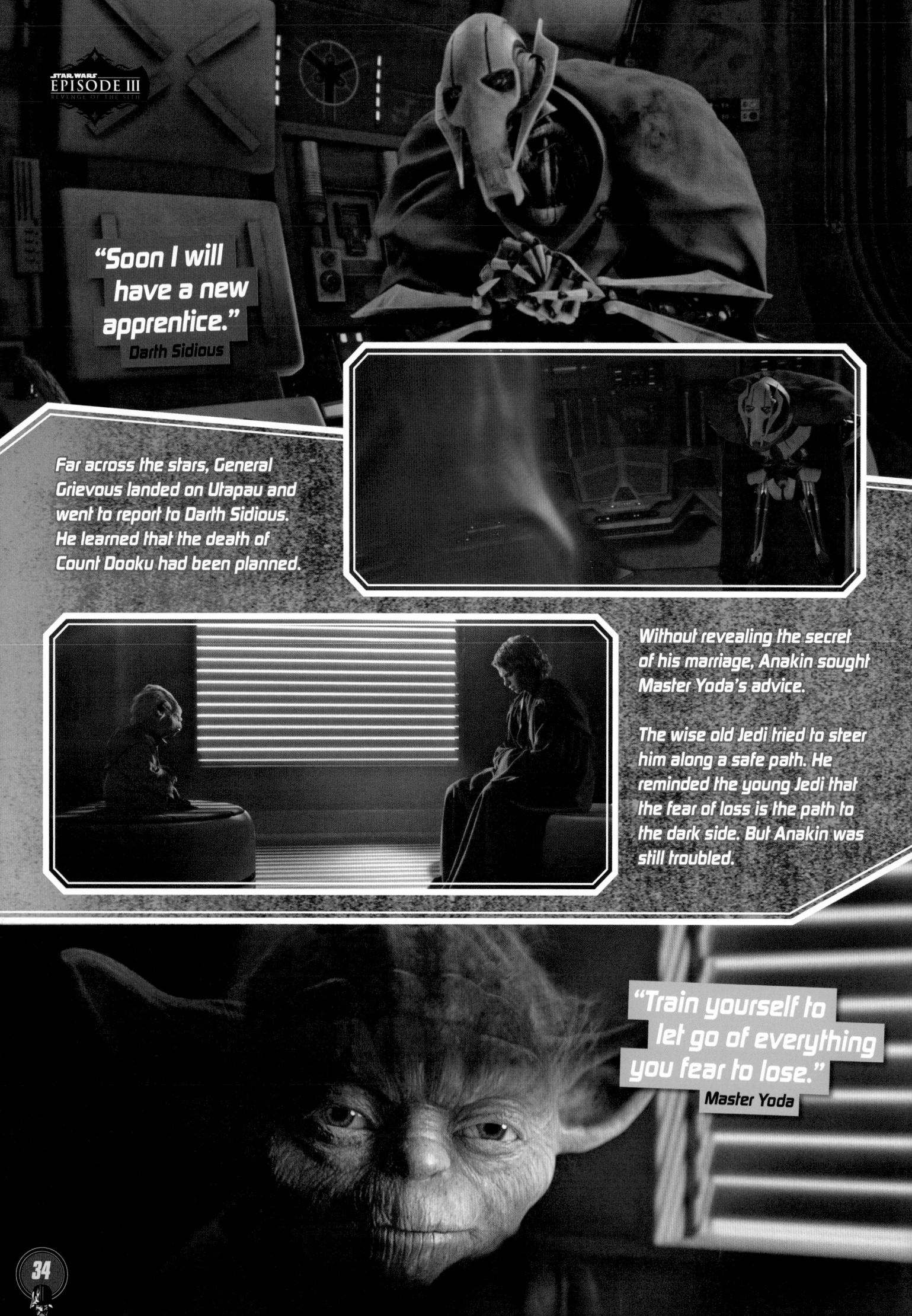

"Soon I will have a new apprentice."
Darth Sidious

Far across the stars, General Grievous landed on Utapau and went to report to Darth Sidious. He learned that the death of Count Dooku had been planned.

Without revealing the secret of his marriage, Anakin sought Master Yoda's advice.

The wise old Jedi tried to steer him along a safe path. He reminded the young Jedi that the fear of loss is the path to the dark side. But Anakin was still troubled.

"Train yourself to let go of everything you fear to lose."
Master Yoda

Meanwhile, the Jedi Council was becoming increasingly worried about the Chancellor's political powers. Sensing that they didn't trust him, Palpatine appointed Anakin as his personal representative on the Council.

The Jedi were not pleased at this turn of events. They refused to grant Anakin the rank of Master.

"Be careful of your friend Palpatine."

Obi-Wan Kenobi

"This is outrageous! It's unfair . . . I'm more powerful than any of you!"

Anakin Skywalker

35

"The dark side of the Force surrounds the Chancellor."
Mace Windu

The Jedi asked Anakin to report on all the Chancellor's dealings. They could sense that something was out of place.

Some of the Senators were starting to doubt the Chancellor too. Padmé was one of them. With Bail Organa, Mon Mothma and several others, she formed an alliance to try to stop Palpatine taking more power.

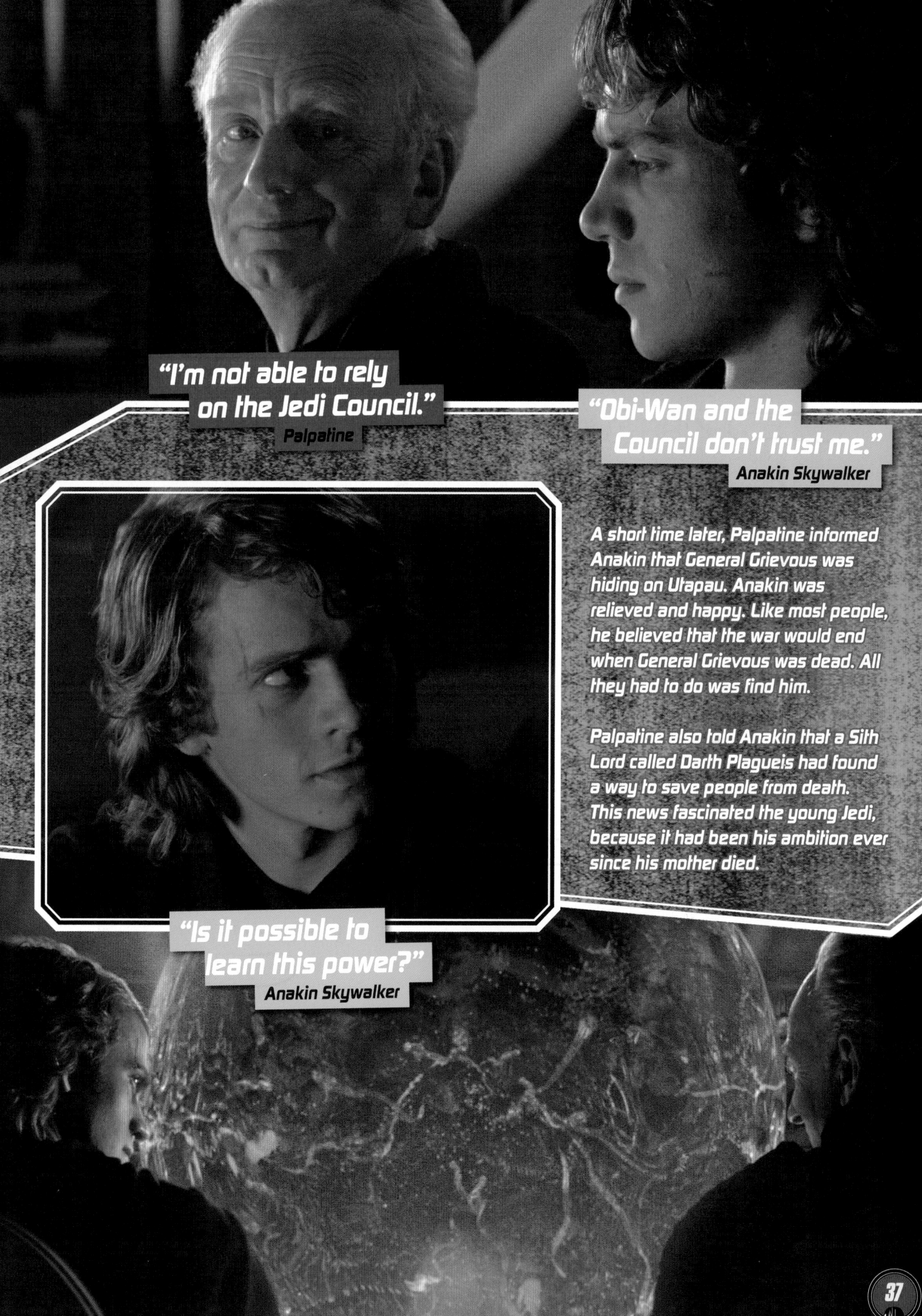

"I'm not able to rely on the Jedi Council."

Palpatine

"Obi-Wan and the Council don't trust me."

Anakin Skywalker

A short time later, Palpatine informed Anakin that General Grievous was hiding on Utapau. Anakin was relieved and happy. Like most people, he believed that the war would end when General Grievous was dead. All they had to do was find him.

Palpatine also told Anakin that a Sith Lord called Darth Plagueis had found a way to save people from death. This news fascinated the young Jedi, because it had been his ambition ever since his mother died.

"Is it possible to learn this power?"

Anakin Skywalker

VILLAINS OF THE CLONE WARS

While the Clone Wars raged across the galaxy, there were some who enjoyed the destruction and chaos it caused. Many benefited from the misery of others.

JABBA THE HUTT

This repulsive and corrupt gangster was involved in every criminal activity he could find. Piracy, slavery, gambling – nothing was beneath him. He was based on Tatooine, where he controlled most of the cities, towns and spaceports.

Jabba aimed to become the most powerful crime lord in the Outer Rim, and although he supported the Republic, he had no real loyalties. He would do anything that helped his business interests. For some, the Clone Wars were a dark and unhappy time. But for Jabba the Hutt, they were just another way of making money.

DID YOU KNOW ★★★★

Jabba's son Rotta was kidnapped during the Clone Wars and rescued by the Jedi.

DID YOU KNOW ★★★★

Count Dooku was one of the Lost Twenty – the few Jedi Masters who had left the Order.

COUNT DOOKU

Although he had once been a powerful Jedi, Count Dooku turned to the dark side and embraced the ways of the Sith. Following the orders of Darth Sidious, he was greatly responsible for the start of the Clone Wars. He recruited agents to help him make trouble across the galaxy, and he also tempted the greedy commerce barons to join the Separatist cause.

During the Clone Wars, Count Dooku encouraged and created enemies of the Republic. One of his greatest successes was in training the beautiful assassin Asajj Ventress. He did everything he could to weaken and discredit the Jedi, and without him it is possible that the Clone Wars would never have started.

GENERAL GRIEVOUS

The Confederacy of Independent Systems needed someone to lead their massive droid army. They chose a military mastermind who was free of kindness or goodness. General Grievous was a terrifying combination of flesh and metal, and he struck fear into the hearts of his enemies.

Throughout the Clone Wars, his reputation grew as a vicious and cunning killer. He hunted Jedi for sport and kept their lightsabers as trophies. Of all the villains of the Clone Wars, General Grievous must surely rate as the most terrifying.

DID YOU KNOW Some of the medical droids who transformed General Grievous into a cyborg later repaired what remained of Darth Vader's human body.

DID YOU KNOW Sidious's lightsaber had an aurodium cap and blade emitter and a phrik alloy casing.

DARTH SIDIOUS

Although very few knew of his existence, Darth Sidious was surely the greatest villain of the Clone Wars. From the shadows of Coruscant he masterminded the fall of the Republic and the destruction of the Jedi.

Using his Sith powers and his ability to detect the weaknesses of others, Darth Sidious exploited commercial leaders and Jedi Knights alike. He made the rift between the Republic and the Separatists worse, even when - in his guise as Palpatine - he seemed to be encouraging peace.

He pretended to care for those who obeyed him, his cold heart loved nothing and no one except himself.

NUTE GUNRAY

The Viceroy of the Trade Federation didn't care about democracy or the welfare of ordinary citizens. He joined the Separatist movement because he thought it would make him richer. Gunray was a chancer who would do anything to make more money. He had no respect for those who worked for him or for the galaxy.

During the Clone Wars, he followed the orders of Darth Sidious and had the protection of General Grievous. He sent his droid army into battle and was the cause of many violent deaths. It was fitting that his own death, at the hands of Darth Vader, was also cruel and violent.

DID YOU KNOW Nute Gunray escaped four trials before the Supreme Court and continued to serve as a viceroy.

FAST FACTS

SPECIES: Human

HOMEWORLD: Tatooine

HEIGHT: 1.85m

LOYALTY: Jedi

FRIENDS: Obi-Wan Kenobi, Padmé Amidala, Senator Palpatine

ENEMIES: Count Dooku

VEHICLE

NAME: ETA-2 Jedi Starfighter

SIZE: 5.47m

TOP SPEED: 1500 kph

WEAPONS: 2 dual laser cannons, 2 ion cannons

COLOUR: Yellow and grey

"If you're not with me, then you're my enemy."

ANAKIN SKYWALKER

Anakin is a hero throughout the galaxy, thanks to his amazing exploits on the front lines of the Clone Wars. He has carried out daring rescues, defended entire planets and faced many dangerous enemies.

The Force is stronger than ever with him. However, the qualities that have made him a hero are also the qualities that worry the Jedi Council. He is headstrong, passionate and impulsive.

Although it goes against the Jedi Code, Anakin has married Padmé Amidala in secret. He is also good friends with Supreme Chancellor Palpatine, while the other Jedi keep their distance.

Anakin is motivated by love, but sometimes his actions have unexpected consequences – especially when he fails to control his temper. Many Jedi believe that he is the Chosen One, destined to bring balance to the Force. But not even Master Yoda can foresee how this might happen.

Yoda

CLONE TROOPER

MEMORY SKETCH

A Jedi should be able to perfectly recall anyone he has met. Practise your drawing skills by completing these pictures from memory. Take your time to do your best. Let the Force guide you.

Chewbacca

GENERAL GRIEVOUS

41

PADAWAN'S QUIZ

What have you learned from your Jedi studies, young Padawan? Are you ready to begin the next stage of discovery? Answer these questions and find out which Jedi Master will guide you forward.

1 The dark side of the Force is represented by:

- A The Sith ✓
- B The Separatists
- C The Republic

2 Which of these does Yoda say is a path to the dark side?

- A The fear of battle
- B The fear of the Sith
- C The fear of loss ✓

3 What is the role of the Jedi in the galaxy?

- A Super soldiers ✗
- B Peacekeepers
- C Magicians

4 A Padawan's lightsaber is made by:

- A Geonosians
- B The Padawan ✗
- C The Padawan's Jedi Master

5 Complete this important Jedi philosophy: 'There is no death, there is only _____'

- A the Force ✓
- B life
- C knowledge

6 What is the best way to improve yourself as a Jedi?

- A Following your heart
- P Training and learning ✓
- C Lightsaber duelling

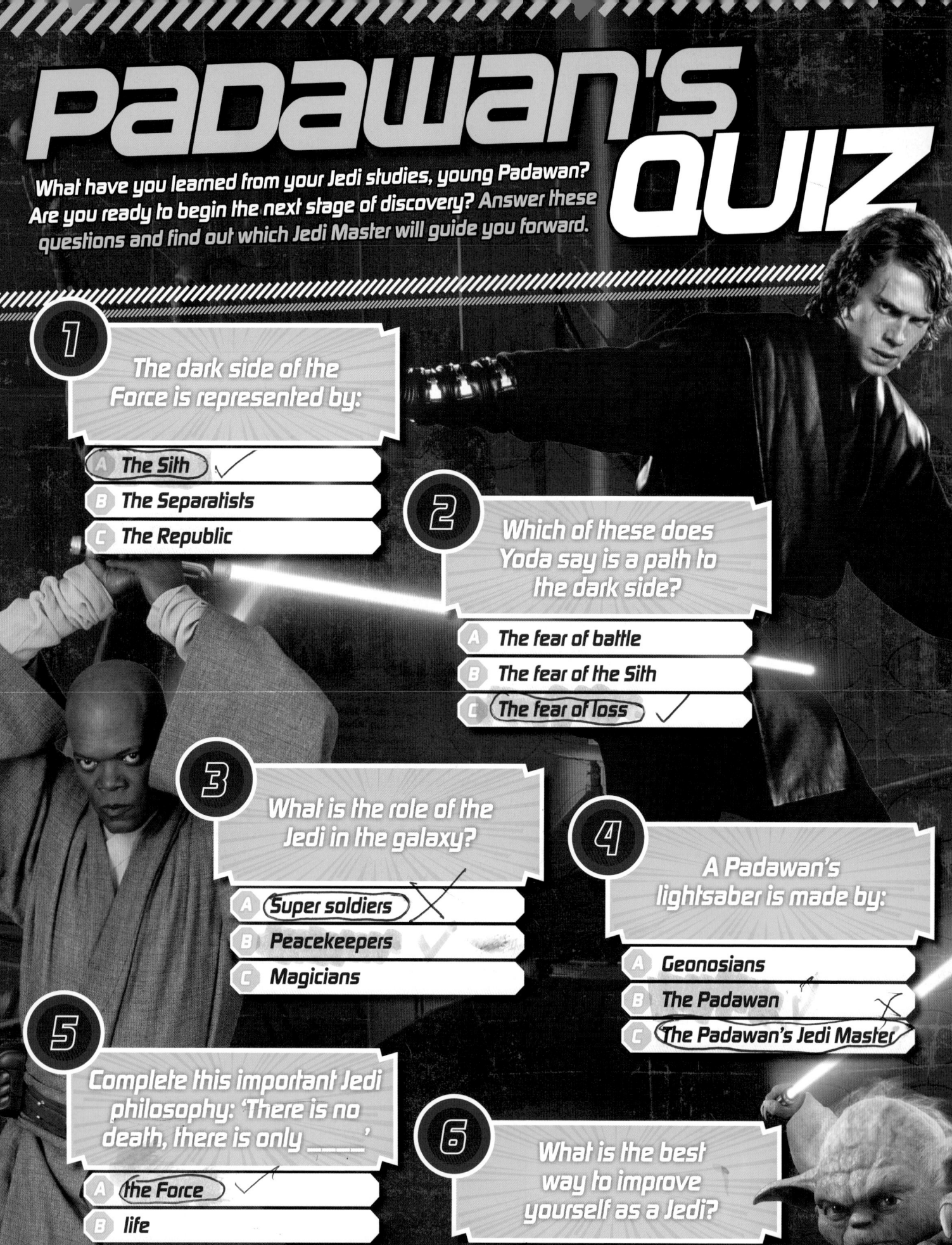

7 The Jedi respect all life in any form. Do you ever try to avoid treading on insects as you walk along?

A Never ✗
B Occasionally
C Always ✓

8 Jedi can only command an army of:

A life forms
B droids
C Jedi ✗

9 Jedi are not allowed to:

A fight
B lie
C marry ✗✓

10 Not every Jedi Knight becomes a Master. What makes a Jedi suitable to become a Master?

A Influential friends in important jobs
B Personal achievements and abilities
C Personal ambition ✓

Check your answers and add up your score. Then find out who your Jedi Master will be!

8 - 10

You have developed much wisdom in your years as a youngling. Now you will join Master Obi-Wan Kenobi to continue your training as a Padawan.

5 - 7

You have done well, but you need a Master who will be disciplined and traditional. Mace Windu will guide your next steps.

1 - 4

You still have much to learn, young one. You will continue to be taught by Master Yoda until you are ready to leave the Temple.

YOUR SCORE

6

43

The Separatists have developed a secret code to help them
share information without the Jedi's knowledge.
Using the code above, can you figure out what these messages say?

message 1

... *wants a bounty hunter to assassinate* ...

message 2

message 3

message 4

message 5

message 6

FAST FACTS

SPECIES: Human

HOMEWORLD: Naboo

HEIGHT: 1.65m

LOYALTY: Jedi Council

FRIENDS: Anakin Skywalker, Obi-Wan Kenobi, Jar Jar Binks

ENEMIES: Nute Gunray, Count Dooku

VEHICLE

NAME: Naboo Star Skiff

SIZE: 29.2m

MANUFACTURER: Theed Palace Space Vessel Engineering Corps

WEAPONS: 2 top-mounted laser cannons

SPECIAL FEATURES: Chromium sheath, medical suite

PADMÉ AMIDALA

Padmé Amidala may be young, but in her short life she has achieved more than many manage in a lifetime. She has reigned as the Queen of Naboo, made peace with the Gungans and served as a Senator for her planet. Now she is also the secret wife of a Jedi Knight.

Padmé has a gentle heart and a sweet nature, and she is also capable of great strength. The first time that Anakin Skywalker laid eyes on her, he thought that she was an angel. Since then he has come to rely on her clear-sightedness, her honesty and her determination.

"Anakin, you're breaking my heart!"

HEROES OF THE CLONE WARS

The Clone Wars were a dark time for ordinary citizens. Those who didn't support the Separatists were always in danger of attack or occupation. The Jedi generals led the clone army to defend and protect citizens, and those they saved will never forget them.

The Clone Wars produced heroes that became legends in their own time. The members of the Jedi Council were well-known throughout the galaxy, and must never be forgotten . . .

YODA

Master Yoda was one of the senior members of the Council. His age and wisdom inspired confidence in his friends and fear in his enemies.

KI-ADI-MUNDI

Another of the senior members of the Council, Ki-Adi-Mundi was trained by Master Yoda. He was a natural leader, and at the start of the Clone Wars he commanded clone trooper forces on Lianna and Hypori.

MACE WINDU

Mace Windu was a senior member of the Council. He had a light-hearted sense of humour, but after the Battle of Naboo he wasn't seen to smile.

SHAAK TI

Shaak Ti was a Togruta, with colorful patterns on her flexible lekku. Her hollow montrals could ultrasonically sense space. She came from the planet Shili, and was very independent. She practiced two lightsaber techniques – Makashi and Ataru.

PLO KOON

This brave warrior was descended from a long line of Jedi Knights. He was a Kel Dor from Dorin, and had to wear protective goggles and an antiox mask whenever he was on Coruscant.

STASS ALLIE

An experienced warrior who fought in the Battle of Geonosis. However, as the Clone Wars went on she became more interested in the healing arts practised by the Circle of Jedi Healers.

KIT FISTO

Kit Fisto came from the Sabilon region of Glee Anselm. He could live in air or water, and his special sense of smell could detect the emotions of others. Kit Fisto was one of the team that went to arrest Chancellor Palpatine, and fell under the Sith Lord's blade.

SAESEE TIIN

Saesee Tiin was a skilled starfighter pilot and well known for his daring space battles. He had natural telepathic abilities and a strong connection to the Force, which meant he could focus his mind even when he was travelling at staggering speeds.

COLEMAN KCAJ

Coleman Kcaj was an Ongree member of the Jedi Council. He was at the Galaxies Opera House during the performance of Squid Lake, when Anakin Skywalker went to tell Chancellor Palpatine news of General Grievous.

ANAKIN SKYWALKER

In the last days of the Clone Wars, Chancellor Palpatine insisted that Anakin should join the Jedi Council. He wanted to find out what the Jedi were saying, and he hoped that Anakin would spy for him. The other Jedi were suspicious of the Chancellor's motives, and refused to grant Anakin the status of Master. This was one of many ways in which the Chancellor divided Anakin from his friends.

AGEN KOLAR

This Zabrak Jedi was known to strike first and ask questions later. He was a stern warrior and was one of the first to face Darth Sidious. His skills as a fighter were impressive, but he was no match for the Sith Lord's lightning-fast reflexes.

OBI-WAN KENOBI

Master Kenobi was dedicated to the Jedi Order, and a bold warrior. He was cautious by nature, and General Grievous called him 'the negotiator'. Obi-Wan Kenobi was one of the few Jedi who survived Order 66, and his fate was linked forever with the destiny of the galaxy.

STAR WARS™
EPISODE III
REVENGE OF THE SITH

PART 2

With the end of the Clone Wars in sight at last, Master Yoda set a course for Kashyyyk to fight alongside the Wookiees. .

Obi-Wan was sent to find General Grievous on Utapau. He confronted the vicious cyborg and they fought with all the skill they possessed.

As clone troopers attacked the droid army, Obi-Wan chased General Grievous across the planet. At last he fired a blaster into the cyborg's stomach, and the General exploded from the inside out.

"You fool. I have been trained in your Jedi arts by Count Dooku himself."
General Grievous

"You forget I trained the Jedi that defeated Count Dooku!"
Obi-Wan Kenobi

Meanwhile, Padmé and five other senators visited Chancellor Palpatine. They wanted reassurance that he was trying to end the war, and that the Republic would return to democracy.

The Chancellor found it hard to hide his impatience, and Padmé was frustrated.

"I will do what is right; that should be enough for your committee."
Palpatine

Palpatine's answers did not satisfy the senators. Anakin felt upset and confused to see those he trusted completely turning on each other.

Finally, Palpatine sensed that the time had come to reveal his true nature to Anakin. He revealed that he was the Sith Lord Darth Sidious.

"Perhaps you'll reconsider and help me rule the galaxy for the good of all."
Palpatine

"You're a Sith Lord!"
Anakin Skywalker

The young Jedi was horrified and decided to turn him over to the Jedi Council. While he went to fetch Mace Windu, the Chancellor waited patiently. He felt confident that the dark side would overpower the young man.

Anakin told Mace Windu what he had discovered, but he felt uneasy. Palpatine had tempted him with the knowledge of how to stop death. What if this was his only chance to save Padmé?

"We must move quickly if the Jedi Order is to survive."
Mace Windu

"In the name of the Galactic Senate of the Republic, you are under arrest, Chancellor."
Mace Windu

The Jedi Master went to arrest the Chancellor with three other Jedi. Against Mace Windu's orders, Anakin followed him to the Chancellor's office.

Palpatine quickly killed Agen Kolar, Kit Fisto and Saesee Tiin. But Mace Windu was a great warrior, and after a fierce battle he forced Palpatine to drop his sword.

Anakin arrived to find his mentor losing the fight.

"You old fool. The oppression of the Sith will never return."
Mace Windu

52

> "Your plot to regain control of the Republic is over . . . you have lost."
>
> Mace Windu

Palpatine used Force lightning, but Mace Windu blocked it and turned it back on the Chancellor. His face twisted and distorted.

But Mace Windu hadn't bargained for the doubts that Palpatine had placed in Anakin's mind.

Anakin realised that Mace Windu was going to kill the Chancellor, and fear bubbled up inside him.

> "He must live . . . I need him!"
>
> Anakin Skywalker

> "Anakin, I am your pathway to power. I have the power to save the one you love."
>
> Palpatine

STAR WARS
EPISODE III
REVENGE OF THE SITH

As the Jedi Master raised his lightsaber, Anakin lunged forward and cut Mace's hand. Mace stared at Anakin in shock, and Palpatine's yellow eyes filled with glee. He blasted Mace Windu with the full force of his powers.

"You are fulfilling your destiny, Anakin."
Palpatine

Anakin watched in horror as the Jedi Master was flung out of the window to his death.

Palpatine's cruel laughter filled the room.

Anakin felt numb, but he couldn't turn back now. All he cared about was finding a way to save Padmé's life. The Chancellor now had complete control over him.

Anakin fell to his knees.

"What have I done?"
Anakin Skywalker

"The Force is strong with you. A powerful Sith you will become. Henceforth, you shall be known as Darth Vader."
Palpatine

FAST FACTS

SPECIES: Kaleesh

HOMEWORLD: Kalee

HEIGHT: 1.83–2.24m (variable)

LOYALTY: Confederacy of Independent Systems

FRIENDS: Count Dooku, Darth Sidious

ENEMIES: Jedi Order

VEHICLE

NAME: Invisible Hand (Trade Federation cruiser)

SIZE: 1,088m

TOP SPEED: 2,000 kph

PROPULSION: 4 Nubian Creveld 4 radial ion drives

CREW: 1 pilot, 1 astromech droid

WEAPONS: 14 quad turbolaser turrets, 34 dual laser cannons, 2 ion cannons, 12 point-defence ion cannons, 102 proton torpedo tubes

COMPLEMENT: 120 droid tri-fighters, 120 droid Vulture fighters, 160 MTTs (Multi Troop Transports), 280 assorted droid armoured vehicles

"Crush them! Make them suffer!"

GENERAL GRIEVOUS

General Grievous is a gifted warmonger, without a scrap of pity for those he fights or those he leads. His body itself is a weapon, and he is the nightmare face of the enemy.

The General was born Qymaen Jai Sheelal, a Kaleesh champion who fought in the Huk War. He was betrayed by his ally San Hill and struck down, but he did not die. Instead he was transformed into a cyborg on the planet of Geonosis.

Grievous trained with Count Dooku, and became skilled at duelling with the lightsaber. He takes great delight in fighting and killing Jedi warriors, and his cunning and combat style make him almost unbeatable.

WORDSEARCH

TEN JEDI NAMES ARE HIDDEN IN THIS GRID.
CAN YOU FIND THEM ALL?
AS YOU FIND EACH ONE, PUT A TICK
NEXT TO THEM IN THE LIST BELOW.

```
A P T A K K S F L P Z R J A M
F Y L Q Z I L I Q N I K R N A
E Y O O A S T J O X Y A N R B
N L E D K K C F A R L P G T E
L D O Y A O Y I I O P O Y A W
E Z N A E T O E K S O L F X I
S Q H B I S T N R W T R E T D
U S S M L N E U O U E O W U N
Q D I Q L G E P T S U Z T X U
S A S R A M U D N I W E C A M
H A R P S S L X T Q S S T O I
I Q Y A S A P V C V E T Q V D
C T P J A C K N A M E L O C A
A N I I T Z R Q T X T Y L I I
D G O I S A E S E E T I I N K
```

- [ ] YODA
- [ ] KI-ADI-MUNDI
- [ ] MACE WINDU
- [ ] PLO KOON
- [ ] STASS ALLIE
- [ ] SHAAK TI
- [ ] KIT FISTO
- [ ] SAESEE TIIN
- [ ] COLEMAN KCAJ
- [ ] AGEN KOLAR

HOW TO DRAW
Padmé Amidala

Follow these simple steps to learn how to draw the beautiful young Senator.

STEP 1

Stick figure:
First you get the proper position and proportions by drawing a simple stick figure.

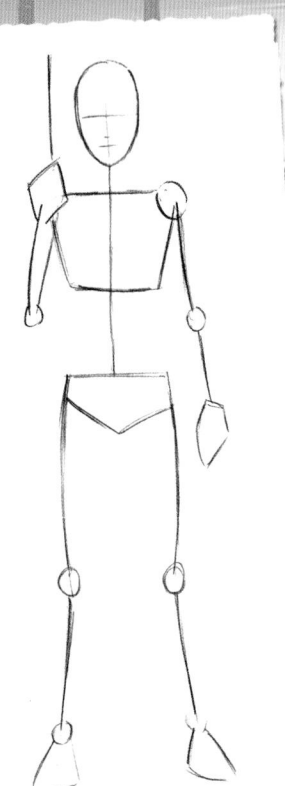

STEP 2

Fleshinig out:
Then you build the body (flesh it out) by adding cylinders.

STEP 3

Details:
Now work into your construction lines and add all the fiddly details.

STEP 4

Ink:
Finally, draw a neat ink line over you drawing. Once the ink has dried, erase the pencil underneath.

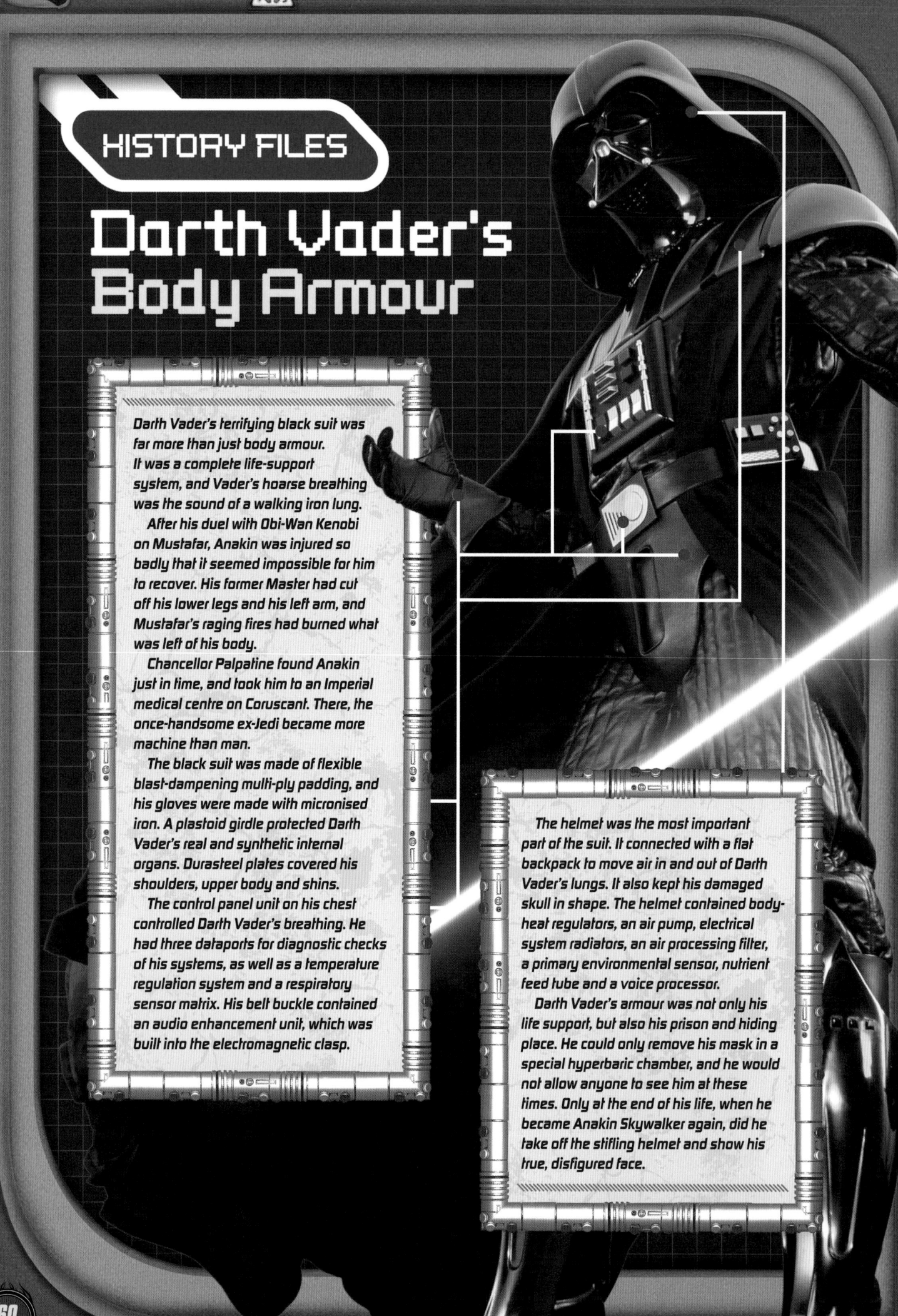

Darth Vader's Body Armour

Darth Vader's terrifying black suit was far more than just body armour. It was a complete life-support system, and Vader's hoarse breathing was the sound of a walking iron lung.

After his duel with Obi-Wan Kenobi on Mustafar, Anakin was injured so badly that it seemed impossible for him to recover. His former Master had cut off his lower legs and his left arm, and Mustafar's raging fires had burned what was left of his body.

Chancellor Palpatine found Anakin just in time, and took him to an Imperial medical centre on Coruscant. There, the once-handsome ex-Jedi became more machine than man.

The black suit was made of flexible blast-dampening multi-ply padding, and his gloves were made with micronised iron. A plastoid girdle protected Darth Vader's real and synthetic internal organs. Durasteel plates covered his shoulders, upper body and shins.

The control panel unit on his chest controlled Darth Vader's breathing. He had three dataports for diagnostic checks of his systems, as well as a temperature regulation system and a respiratory sensor matrix. His belt buckle contained an audio enhancement unit, which was built into the electromagnetic clasp.

The helmet was the most important part of the suit. It connected with a flat backpack to move air in and out of Darth Vader's lungs. It also kept his damaged skull in shape. The helmet contained body-heat regulators, an air pump, electrical system radiators, an air processing filter, a primary environmental sensor, nutrient feed tube and a voice processor.

Darth Vader's armour was not only his life support, but also his prison and hiding place. He could only remove his mask in a special hyperbaric chamber, and he would not allow anyone to see him at these times. Only at the end of his life, when he became Anakin Skywalker again, did he take off the stifling helmet and show his true, disfigured face.

galaxy map

PADMÉ MUST FOLLOW ANAKIN TO MUSTAFAR, AND TRY TO SAVE HIM FROM HIMSELF. HELP HER BY PLOTTING HER ROUTE ACROSS THE GALAXY.

DESIGN a HERO

Heroes come in all shapes and sizes. Use your imagination to create a new hero for the clone wars. Draw and colour your hero's picture, and then fill in their details.

NAME: ....

AGE: ....

GENDER: ....

SPECIES: ....

HOMEWORLD: ....

HEIGHT: ....

LOYALTY: ....

WEAPON: ....

VEHICLE: ....

TRAINED BY: ....

FRIENDS: ....

ENEMIES: ....

MOST HEROIC MOMENT: ....

....

....

....

CROSSWORD SPIRAL

A Jedi must learn to tackle familiar problems in a new way. Instead of a grid, this crossword puzzle is in a spiral form. The last letter of each answer is the first letter of the next answer. Start in the centre and keep going until you have reached the end of the spiral.

1. A famous Wookiee.

2. Darth Vader's first name.

3. The Chancellor's home planet.

4. The Jedi who found the clone army on Kamino.

5. Darth Maul's personal starship is called the Sith _____.

6. The Galaxy is ruled by the Galactic _____.

7. The location of the Jedi Temple.

8. The planet where Qui-Gon Jinn first saw Darth Maul.

9. The Chancellor will one day call himself by this title.

FAST FACTS

SPECIES: Human

HOMEWORLD: Alderaan

HEIGHT: 1.91m

LOYALTY: Galactic Senate

FRIENDS: Padmé Amidala, Obi-Wan Kenobi, Breha Organa

ENEMIES: Chancellor Palpatine

VEHICLE

NAME: Narglatch XJ-2 airspeeder

SIZE: 5.9m

SPECIAL ABILITIES: Bail Organa restored and modified his classic airspeeder in times of peace. He no longer has time for this hobby, but he keeps the airspeeder. It is registered under a false name, and Bail thinks that there may come a time when he needs to travel in secret.

"The Chancellor has become an enemy of democracy."

BAIL ORGANA

Senator Bail Organa of Alderaan is a loyal senator and a passionate believer in democracy. It brought him great sadness when the Republic had to go to war. His honesty and goodness are unusual among the many corrupt politicians in the Senate. He is a kind man, and he opposes policies that make life harder for the weak and needy.

Since he talked to Finis Valorum, who was suspicious of Palpatine, Bail has been questioning the war effort. He has found out that a lot of information about the war is being hidden from the Senate.

Since Finis Valorum was killed, Bail has kept challenging the war powers that are granted to Palpatine. He can see that Palpatine is almost a dictator. He is sure that the Chancellor is up to no good, and he is ready to risk his life to save democracy.

STAR WARS
EPISODE III
REVENGE OF THE SITH

PART 3

Palpatine had succeeded in turning the Chosen One against the Jedi Order. He told Anakin that he must destroy the Jedi. Only by showing them no mercy could he be strong enough with the dark side to save Padmé.

Following the Chancellor's orders, Anakin went to the Jedi Temple and cut down all the younglings. Then he travelled to the Mustafar system to destroy the Separatists.

"Do what must be done, Lord Vader."
Palpatine

"The remaining Jedi will be hunted down and defeated."

Palpatine

Meanwhile, the Chancellor issued Order 66: kill all Jedi. As soon as the order was activated, the clones turned on their Jedi generals. Only a few Jedi escaped.

The Chancellor told the Senate that the Jedi had been plotting to destroy the Republic. He announced the birth of the Galactic Empire – ruled by him.

Bail Organa rescued Master Yoda and Obi-Wan. They returned to the Jedi Temple in secret, and discovered the terrible truth. Anakin Skywalker had killed those he was supposed to protect.

Obi-Wan and Master Yoda knew that now Anakin had turned to the dark side they had to kill both the Chancellor and his new apprentice.

"I will do what I must."
Obi-Wan Kenobi

Obi-Wan was sure that Padmé knew where to find Anakin. He visited her and tried to find out more, but she would not betray her husband.

Padmé was sickened by the end of democracy, and confused by Anakin's actions. She travelled to Mustafar to find him, and Obi-Wan hid on board her ship.

"At last the Jedi are no more."
Palpatine

Padmé arrived after Anakin had killed the Separatist leaders. The bloodshed of the last few hours had blackened his heart, and the dark side was consuming him.

"I am becoming more powerful than any Jedi has ever been."
Anakin Skywalker

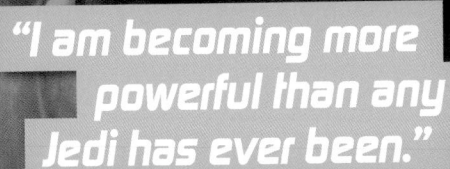

For a short while, Anakin was pleased to see Padmé. But his jealousy and fear quickly made him doubt her. When he saw Obi-Wan, he thought that she had betrayed him. He used the Force to half-choke her, and she fell to the ground in pain and despair.

69

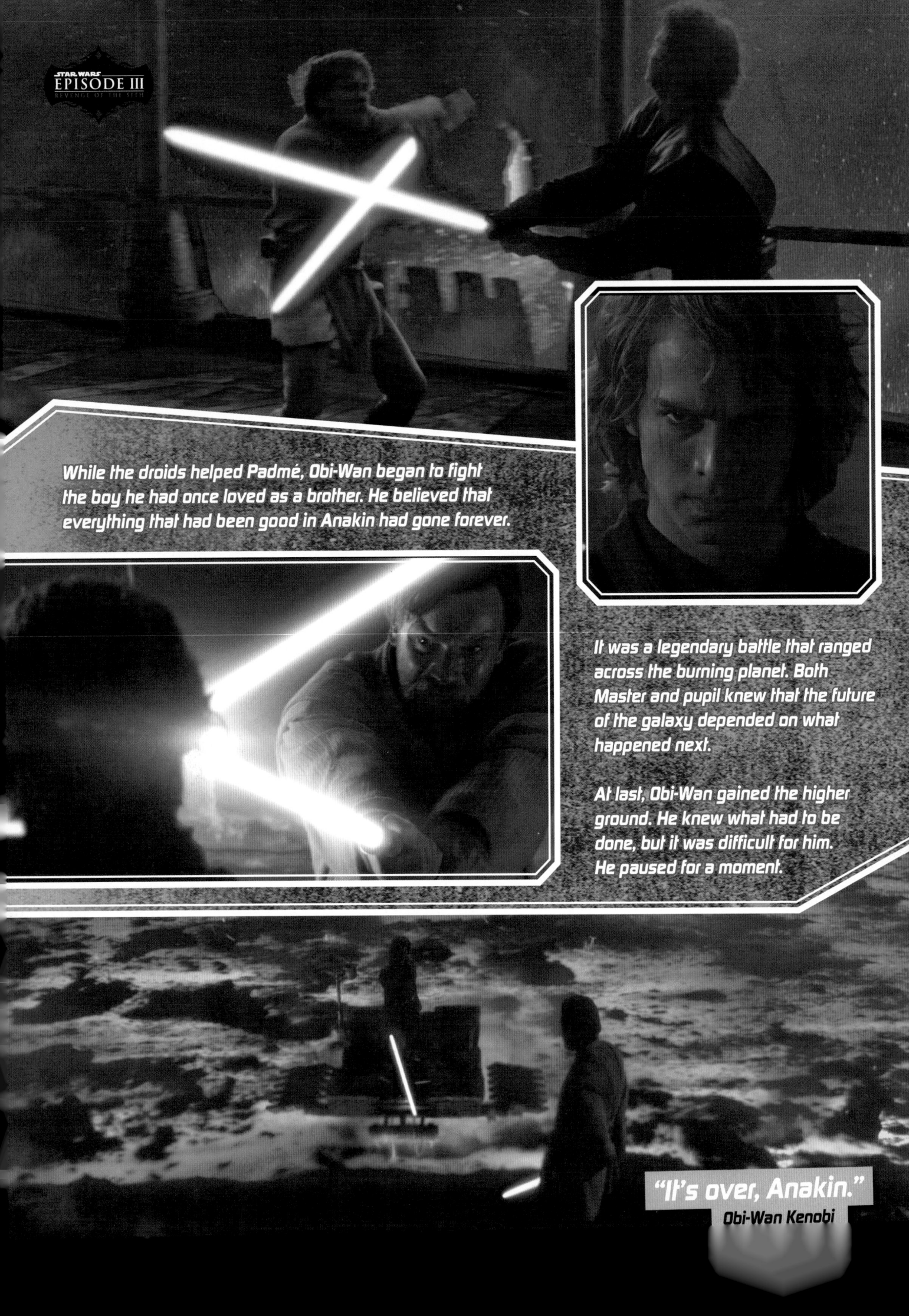

While the droids helped Padmé, Obi-Wan began to fight the boy he had once loved as a brother. He believed that everything that had been good in Anakin had gone forever.

It was a legendary battle that ranged across the burning planet. Both Master and pupil knew that the future of the galaxy depended on what happened next.

At last, Obi-Wan gained the higher ground. He knew what had to be done, but it was difficult for him. He paused for a moment.

"It's over, Anakin."
Obi-Wan Kenobi

Then his lightsaber gleamed through the air, and chopped Anakin's legs off at the knees.

Anakin's love for his Master had turned to blazing hatred. The lava inferno made his clothes burst into flames and he screamed in agony. Obi-Wan turned with a heavy heart and left his Padawan to die. On Coruscant, Yoda's duel with the Chancellor ended in failure. The Jedi were no more.

"You were the Chosen One!"
Obi-Wan Kenobi

71

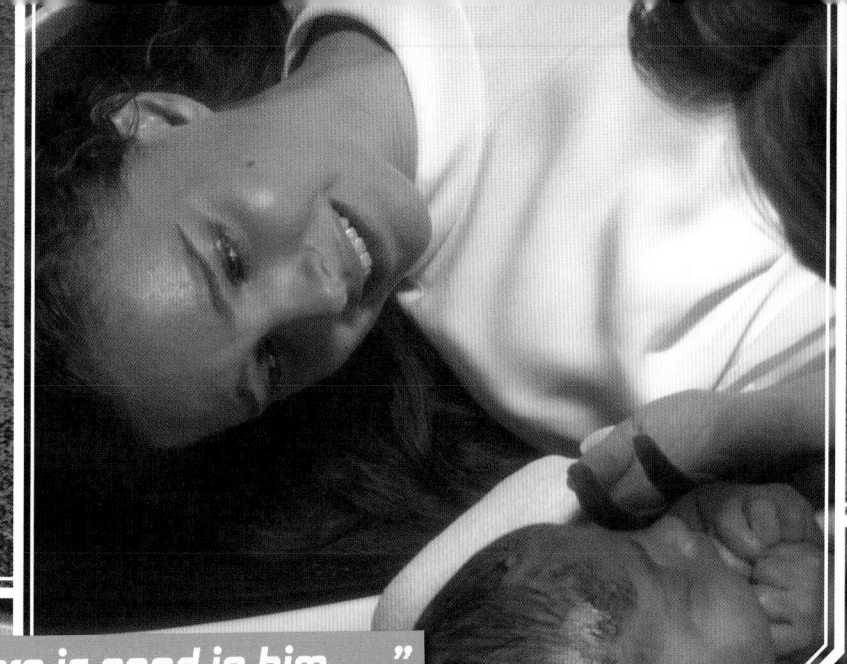

In the midst of Padmé's broken-hearted pain, the time came for her to give birth. Droid medics worked hard to care for her, but she had lost the will to live. Although her twins, Luke and Leia, were born safely, Padmé could not be saved.

"Obi-Wan, there is good in him . . ."
Padmé Amidala

"I sense Lord Vader is in danger."
Palpatine

On Mustafar, Palpatine saved what was left of Anakin's body. In an Imperial rehab centre, medical droids constructed a suit that would keep him alive. When he awoke, he found himself encased in a black prison.

The first thing he heard was that Padmé was dead, and that he had killed her. A low groan came from the chilling mask, and his screams echoed through the centre.

"Strong the Force runs, in the Skywalker line."
Master Yoda

Master Yoda went into hiding on the planet Dagobah, while Padmé's twins were separated and kept secret. Leia went to Alderaan with Bail Organa, while Luke was given to his uncle on Tatooine. Perhaps, one day, these children would bring a new hope to the galaxy . . .

THE JEDI AND THE SITH

Jedi and Sith warriors are like opposite sides of the same coin. Both are born with a strong connection to the Force, both spend years being taught by an experienced Master, and both understand the power of emotions. They are well-matched enemies, for they both use the Force to help them move objects with the mind, leap great distances and even sense the future.

However, while the Jedi value self-control and strive for inner peace and enlightenment, the Sith relish hate and anger. The Jedi accept that life begins and ends, while the Sith fight against nature and destiny. The Jedi are calm, while the Sith are full of rage.

THE JEDI CODE

The Code contains the moral rules that Jedi are expected to follow at all times. It is one of the first things the younglings learn at the Temple.

Jedi are the guardians of peace in the galaxy.
Jedi use their powers to defend and to protect, never to attack others.
Jedi respect all life, in any form.
Jedi serve others rather than ruling over them, for the good of the galaxy.
Jedi seek to improve themselves through knowledge and training.

There is no emotion; there is peace.
There is no ignorance; there is knowledge.
There is no passion; there is serenity.
There is no death; there is only the Force.

A Jedi does not act for personal power or wealth, but seeks knowledge and enlightenment. A Jedi never acts from hatred, anger, fear or aggression but only when calm and at peace with the Force. The Jedi work together for the good of everyone.

In comparison, a Sith seeks individual power. Sith are selfish and greedy, and driven by passion and ambition. The power of the dark side is greater than the power of the light side, and the Sith use their power to hurt and control.

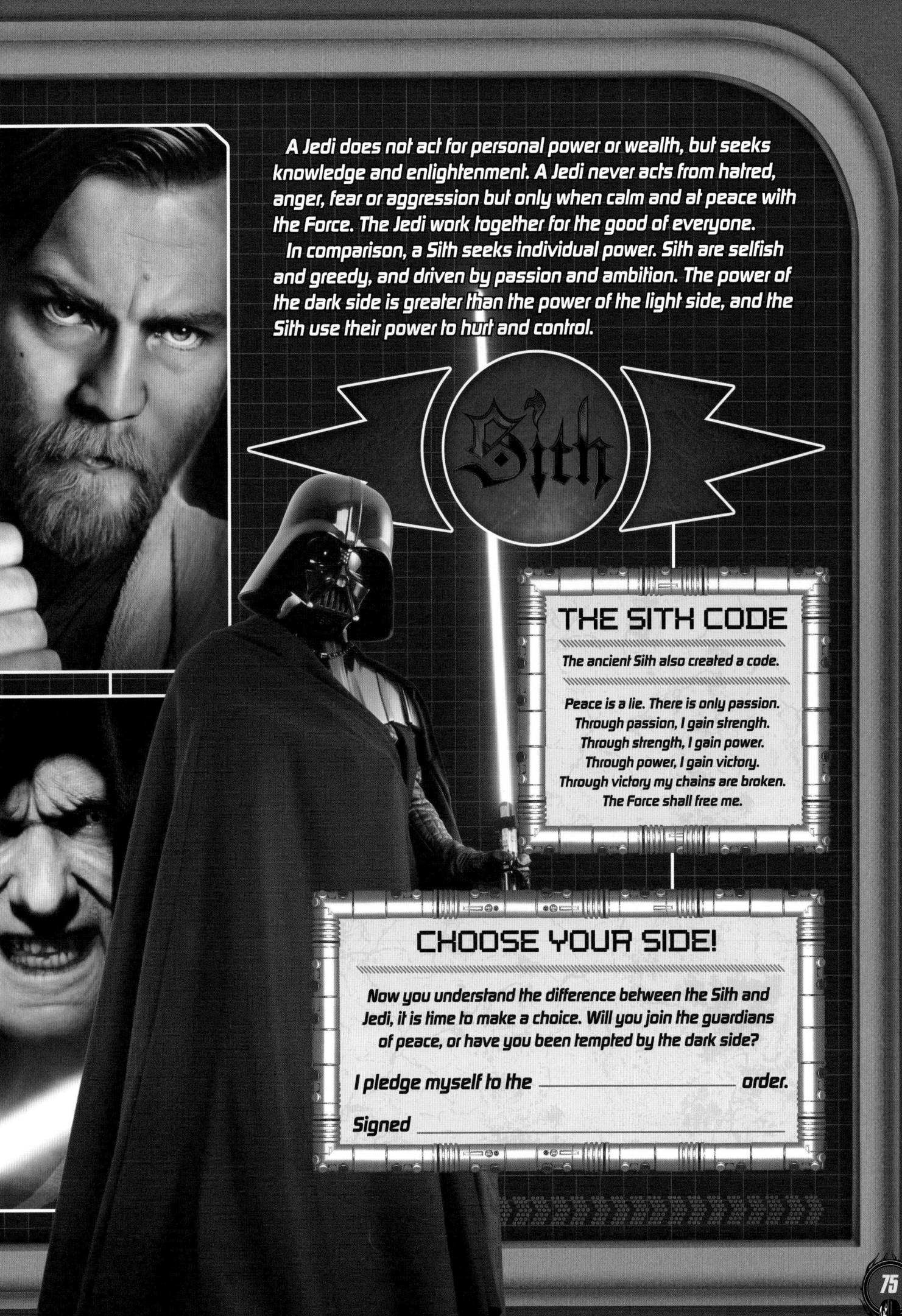

THE SITH CODE

The ancient Sith also created a code.

Peace is a lie. There is only passion.
Through passion, I gain strength.
Through strength, I gain power.
Through power, I gain victory.
Through victory my chains are broken.
The Force shall free me.

CHOOSE YOUR SIDE!

Now you understand the difference between the Sith and Jedi, it is time to make a choice. Will you join the guardians of peace, or have you been tempted by the dark side?

I pledge myself to the _____ order.

Signed _____

FAST FACTS

SPECIES:	*Human*
HOMEWORLD:	*Naboo*
HEIGHT:	*1.78m*
LOYALTY:	*Sith*
FRIENDS:	*Darth Maul, Darth Tyranus, Darth Vader, Darth Plagueis, General Grievous,*
ENEMIES:	*Jedi*

"Everything is going as planned."

DARTH SIDIOUS

This evil genius has a plan to take over the galaxy and crush the Jedi Order. His plan is long-term and ambitious, but he has the intelligence and the cruelty to make it happen. His thirst for power cannot be satisfied.

However, as Senator Palpatine, he has always seemed slow, reliable and honest. He steadily advanced through the political ranks until he was Supreme Chancellor. No one suspects that he is really a Sith Lord.

The Sith have waited for years for a powerful leader to take revenge on the Jedi Order. Darth Sidious was trained by Darth Plagueis, and does not think of himself as evil. He sees himself as a saviour, and has secretly organised a lot of the interplanetary strife that troubles the Republic.

It is in the Sith nature to be secretive, and Palpatine has trained his apprentices and made his plans without the Jedi suspecting a thing.

Now his careful plans are about to pay off.

ANSWERS

PAGE 8
CHARACTER CROSSWORD

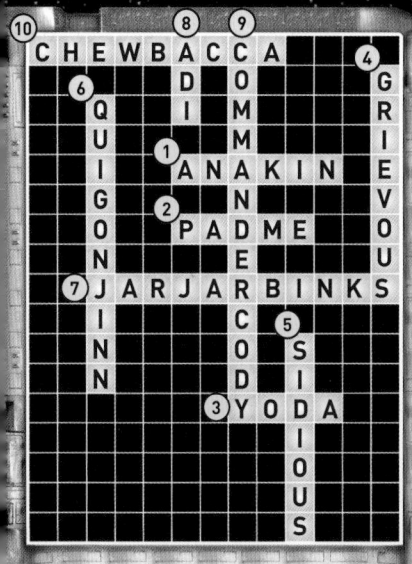

PAGE 8
SPOT THE DIFFERENCE

PAGES 26-27
MAP OF DESTINY

1. QUI-GON JINN
His most famous Padawan will be
Obi-Wan Kenobi.
He will discover a very special boy on
the planet Tatooine.
He will die at the hands of Darth Maul.

2. MACE WINDU
He will sit on the Jedi Council with
Master Yoda.
He will have an unusual purple
lightsaber.
He will die at the hands of Darth Sidious.

3. OBI-WAN KENOBI
He will kill General Grievous.
He will die at the hands of Darth Vader.
He will watch over Padmé Amidala's

---

4. BOBA FETT
He will spend the first years of his life
on Kamino.
He will see Mace Windu kill his father.
He will become a bounty hunter.

5. PADMÉ AMIDALA
She will become Queen of Naboo.
She will get married in secret.
Her daughter will be brought up by
Bail Organa.

6. BAIL ORGANA
He will help to save the lives of
several Jedi.
He will help Qui-Gon Jinn's Padawan
after Order 66.
He will die when his planet explodes.

7. YODA
He will lose a battle with Darth Sidious.
He will train Anakin Skywalker's son to
be a Jedi.
He will become one with the Force on
the planet of Dagobah.

8. ANAKIN SKYWALKER
He will bring balance to the Force.
He will help stop an assassin sent by
Boba Fett's father.
He will kill the younglings in the
Temple.

PAGE 28
EYE-DENTITY PARADE

1. Jar Jar Binks
2. Padmé Amidala
3. General Grievous
4. Count Dooku
5. Poggle the Lesser
6. Chewbacca

PAGES 42-43
PADAWAN'S QUIZ

| 1.A | 2.C | 3.B | 4.B | 5.A |
| 6.B | 7.C | 8.A | 9.C | 10.B |

PAGE 44 - CODE BREAKER

1. Nute Gunray wants a bounty hunter to
assassinate Padmé Amidala.
2. General Grievous will protect all
Separatist leaders.
3. Count Dooku is a Sith Lord.
4. Obey all orders from Darth Sidious.
5. Kill Anakin Skywalker.
6. Count Dooku will kidnap Chancellor

PAGE 57 - WORDSEARCH

PAGE 61 - GALAXY MAP

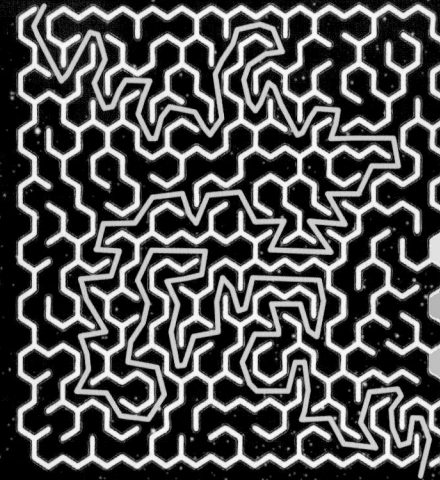

PAGE 64
CROSSWORD SPIRAL

1. Chewbacca
2. Anakin
3. Naboo
4. Obi-Wan Kenobi
5. Infiltrator
6. Republic
7. Coruscant
8. Tatooine
9. Emperor

DROID ARMY

The ten Droids are hidden in pages:
11, 22, 27, 33, 44, 47, 54, 58, 62, 74

Star Wars™ Annual 2014

STAR WARS™

OFFICIAL

Annual 2014

FREE MASK INSIDE

NEW FOR 2013
FREE MASK INSIDE ANNUAL

Pedigree

Visit **Pedigreebooks.com** to find out more on this year's *Star Wars™* Annual, scan with your mobile device to learn more.

Visit www.pedigreebooks.com

Pedigree Books, Beech Hill House, Walnut Gardens, Exeter EX4 4DH